this book belongs to :

Everything Has A Process

Remember the energy you sent out,

is the energy you'll get back

Date: _ _ _ _ _ _ _ _ _ _ _ _

Step 1: What is your current situation?

Step 2: What are the positives and negative?

Step 3: How does that make you feel?

Step 4: How can the situation be improved?

Date:_ _ _ _ _ _ _ _ _ _ _

Step 1: What is your current situation?

Step 2: What are the positives and negative?

Step 3: How does that make you feel?

Step 4: How can the situation be improved?

Date:_ _ _ _ _ _ _ _ _ _ _

Step 1: What is your current situation?

Step 2: What are the positives and negative?

Step 3: How does that make you feel?

Step 4: How can the situation be improved?

Step 1: What is your current situation?

Step 2: What are the positives and negative?

Step 3: How does that make you feel?

Step 4: How can the situation be improved?

Step 1: What is your current situation?

Step 2: What are the positives and negative?

Step 3: How does that make you feel?

Step 4: How can the situation be improved?

Step 1: What is your current situation?

Step 2: What are the positives and negative?

Step 3: How does that make you feel?

Step 4: How can the situation be improved?

Date:_ _ _ _ _ _ _ _ _ _ _

Step 1: What is your current situation?

Step 2: What are the positives and negative?

Step 3: How does that make you feel?

Step 4: How can the situation be improved?

Step 1: What is your current situation?

Step 2: What are the positives and negative?

Step 3: How does that make you feel?

Step 4: How can the situation be improved?

Date:_ _ _ _ _ _ _ _ _ _ _

Step 1: What is your current situation?

Step 2: What are the positives and negative?

Step 3: How does that make you feel?

Step 4: How can the situation be improved?

Step 1: What is your current situation?

Step 2: What are the positives and negative?

Step 3: How does that make you feel?

Step 4: How can the situation be improved?

Date: _ _ _ _ _ _ _ _ _ _ _ _

Step 1: What is your current situation?

Step 2: What are the positives and negative?

Step 3: How does that make you feel?

Step 4: How can the situation be improved?

Date:_ _ _ _ _ _ _ _ _ _ _ _

Step 1: What is your current situation?

Step 2: What are the positives and negative?

Step 3: How does that make you feel?

Step 4: How can the situation be improved?

Date: _ _ _ _ _ _ _ _ _ _ _ _

Step 1: What is your current situation?

Step 2: What are the positives and negative?

Step 3: How does that make you feel?

Step 4: How can the situation be improved?

Step 1: What is your current situation?

Step 2: What are the positives and negative?

Step 3: How does that make you feel?

Step 4: How can the situation be improved?

Step 1: What is your current situation?

Step 2: What are the positives and negative?

Step 3: How does that make you feel?

Step 4: How can the situation be improved?

Date: _ _ _ _ _ _ _ _ _ _ _ _

Step 1: What is your current situation?

Step 2: What are the positives and negative?

Step 3: How does that make you feel?

Step 4: How can the situation be improved?

Step 1: What is your current situation?

Step 2: What are the positives and negative?

Step 3: How does that make you feel?

Step 4: How can the situation be improved?

Step 1: What is your current situation?

Step 2: What are the positives and negative?

Step 3: How does that make you feel?

Step 4: How can the situation be improved?

Date:__ __ __ __ __ __ __ __ __ __ __

Step 1: What is your current situation?

Step 2: What are the positives and negative?

Step 3: How does that make you feel?

Step 4: How can the situation be improved?

Step 1: What is your current situation?

Step 2: What are the positives and negative?

Step 3: How does that make you feel?

Step 4: How can the situation be improved?

Step 1: What is your current situation?

Step 2: What are the positives and negative?

Step 3: How does that make you feel?

Step 4: How can the situation be improved?

Step 1: What is your current situation?

Step 2: What are the positives and negative?

Step 3: How does that make you feel?

Step 4: How can the situation be improved?

Step 1: What is your current situation?

Step 2: What are the positives and negative?

Step 3: How does that make you feel?

Step 4: How can the situation be improved?

Date: _ _ _ _ _ _ _ _ _ _ _

Step 1: What is your current situation?

Step 2: What are the positives and negative?

Step 3: How does that make you feel?

Step 4: How can the situation be improved?

Date:_ _ _ _ _ _ _ _ _ _ _

Step 1: What is your current situation?

Step 2: What are the positives and negative?

Step 3: How does that make you feel?

Step 4: How can the situation be improved?

Step 1: What is your current situation?

Step 2: What are the positives and negative?

Step 3: How does that make you feel?

Step 4: How can the situation be improved?

Date: _ _ _ _ _ _ _ _ _ _ _

Step 1: What is your current situation?

Step 2: What are the positives and negative?

Step 3: How does that make you feel?

Step 4: How can the situation be improved?

Date:_ _ _ _ _ _ _ _ _ _ _

Step 1: What is your current situation?

Step 2: What are the positives and negative?

Step 3: How does that make you feel?

Step 4: How can the situation be improved?

Date: _ _ _ _ _ _ _ _ _ _ _ _

Step 1: What is your current situation?

Step 2: What are the positives and negative?

Step 3: How does that make you feel?

Step 4: How can the situation be improved?

Step 1: What is your current situation?

Step 2: What are the positives and negative?

Step 3: How does that make you feel?

Step 4: How can the situation be improved?

Step 1: What is your current situation?

Step 2: What are the positives and negative?

Step 3: How does that make you feel?

Step 4: How can the situation be improved?

Step 1: What is your current situation?

Step 2: What are the positives and negative?

Step 3: How does that make you feel?

Step 4: How can the situation be improved?

Date: _ _ _ _ _ _ _ _ _ _ _ _

Step 1: What is your current situation?

Step 2: What are the positives and negative?

Step 3: How does that make you feel?

Step 4: How can the situation be improved?

Step 1: What is your current situation?

Step 2: What are the positives and negative?

Step 3: How does that make you feel?

Step 4: How can the situation be improved?

Date:_ _ _ _ _ _ _ _ _ _ _

Step 1: What is your current situation?

Step 2: What are the positives and negative?

Step 3: How does that make you feel?

Step 4: How can the situation be improved?

Date: _ _ _ _ _ _ _ _ _ _ _

Step 1: What is your current situation?

Step 2: What are the positives and negative?

Step 3: How does that make you feel?

Step 4: How can the situation be improved?

Date: _ _ _ _ _ _ _ _ _ _ _

Step 1: What is your current situation?

Step 2: What are the positives and negative?

Step 3: How does that make you feel?

Step 4: How can the situation be improved?

Step 1: What is your current situation?

Step 2: What are the positives and negative?

Step 3: How does that make you feel?

Step 4: How can the situation be improved?

Date: _ _ _ _ _ _ _ _ _ _ _ _

Step 1: What is your current situation?

Step 2: What are the positives and negative?

Step 3: How does that make you feel?

Step 4: How can the situation be improved?

Step 1: What is your current situation?

Step 2: What are the positives and negative?

Step 3: How does that make you feel?

Step 4: How can the situation be improved?

Date: _ _ _ _ _ _ _ _ _ _ _

Step 1: What is your current situation?

Step 2: What are the positives and negative?

Step 3: How does that make you feel?

Step 4: How can the situation be improved?

Date: _ _ _ _ _ _ _ _ _ _ _ _

Step 1: What is your current situation?

Step 2: What are the positives and negative?

Step 3: How does that make you feel?

Step 4: How can the situation be improved?

Step 1: What is your current situation?

Step 2: What are the positives and negative?

Step 3: How does that make you feel?

Step 4: How can the situation be improved?

Step 1: What is your current situation?

Step 2: What are the positives and negative?

Step 3: How does that make you feel?

Step 4: How can the situation be improved?

Date: _ _ _ _ _ _ _ _ _ _ _

Step 1: What is your current situation?

Step 2: What are the positives and negative?

Step 3: How does that make you feel?

Step 4: How can the situation be improved?

Date:_ _ _ _ _ _ _ _ _ _

Step 1: What is your current situation?

Step 2: What are the positives and negative?

Step 3: How does that make you feel?

Step 4: How can the situation be improved?

Step 1: What is your current situation?

Step 2: What are the positives and negative?

Step 3: How does that make you feel?

Step 4: How can the situation be improved?

Date:_ _ _ _ _ _ _ _ _ _ _

Step 1: What is your current situation?

Step 2: What are the positives and negative?

Step 3: How does that make you feel?

Step 4: How can the situation be improved?

Date: _ _ _ _ _ _ _ _ _ _ _

Step 1: What is your current situation?

Step 2: What are the positives and negative?

Step 3: How does that make you feel?

Step 4: How can the situation be improved?

Date: _ _ _ _ _ _ _ _ _ _ _ _

Step 1: What is your current situation?

Step 2: What are the positives and negative?

Step 3: How does that make you feel?

Step 4: How can the situation be improved?

Date: _ _ _ _ _ _ _ _ _ _ _ _

Step 1: What is your current situation?

Step 2: What are the positives and negative?

Step 3: How does that make you feel?

Step 4: How can the situation be improved?

Step 1: What is your current situation?

Step 2: What are the positives and negative?

Step 3: How does that make you feel?

Step 4: How can the situation be improved?

Date: _ _ _ _ _ _ _ _ _ _ _

Step 1: What is your current situation?

Step 2: What are the positives and negative?

Step 3: How does that make you feel?

Step 4: How can the situation be improved?

Step 1: What is your current situation?

Step 2: What are the positives and negative?

Step 3: How does that make you feel?

Step 4: How can the situation be improved?

Step 1: What is your current situation?

Step 2: What are the positives and negative?

Step 3: How does that make you feel?

Step 4: How can the situation be improved?

Step 1: What is your current situation?

Step 2: What are the positives and negative?

Step 3: How does that make you feel?

Step 4: How can the situation be improved?

Step 1: What is your current situation?

Step 2: What are the positives and negative?

Step 3: How does that make you feel?

Step 4: How can the situation be improved?

Date: _ _ _ _ _ _ _ _ _ _ _ _

Step 1: What is your current situation?

Step 2: What are the positives and negative?

Step 3: How does that make you feel?

Step 4: How can the situation be improved?

Date: _ _ _ _ _ _ _ _ _ _ _ _

Step 1: What is your current situation?

Step 2: What are the positives and negative?

Step 3: How does that make you feel?

Step 4: How can the situation be improved?

Date: _ _ _ _ _ _ _ _ _ _ _

Step 1: What is your current situation?

Step 2: What are the positives and negative?

Step 3: How does that make you feel?

Step 4: How can the situation be improved?

Date: _ _ _ _ _ _ _ _ _ _ _ _

Step 1: What is your current situation?

Step 2: What are the positives and negative?

Step 3: How does that make you feel?

Step 4: How can the situation be improved?

Date: _ _ _ _ _ _ _ _ _ _ _ _

Step 1: What is your current situation?

Step 2: What are the positives and negative?

Step 3: How does that make you feel?

Step 4: How can the situation be improved?

Date: _ _ _ _ _ _ _ _ _ _ _ _

Step 1: What is your current situation?

Step 2: What are the positives and negative?

Step 3: How does that make you feel?

Step 4: How can the situation be improved?

Date:_ _ _ _ _ _ _ _ _ _ _ _

Step 1: What is your current situation?

Step 2: What are the positives and negative?

Step 3: How does that make you feel?

Step 4: How can the situation be improved?

Step 1: What is your current situation?

Step 2: What are the positives and negative?

Step 3: How does that make you feel?

Step 4: How can the situation be improved?

Date: _ _ _ _ _ _ _ _ _ _

Step 1: What is your current situation?

Step 2: What are the positives and negative?

Step 3: How does that make you feel?

Step 4: How can the situation be improved?

Step 1: What is your current situation?

Step 2: What are the positives and negative?

Step 3: How does that make you feel?

Step 4: How can the situation be improved?

Date:_ _ _ _ _ _ _ _ _ _ _

Step 1: What is your current situation?

Step 2: What are the positives and negative?

Step 3: How does that make you feel?

Step 4: How can the situation be improved?

Date: _ _ _ _ _ _ _ _ _ _ _ _

Step 1: What is your current situation?

Step 2: What are the positives and negative?

Step 3: How does that make you feel?

Step 4: How can the situation be improved?

Date: _ _ _ _ _ _ _ _ _ _

Step 1: What is your current situation?

Step 2: What are the positives and negative?

Step 3: How does that make you feel?

Step 4: How can the situation be improved?

Date: _ _ _ _ _ _ _ _ _ _ _ _

Step 1: What is your current situation?

Step 2: What are the positives and negative?

Step 3: How does that make you feel?

Step 4: How can the situation be improved?

Date:_ _ _ _ _ _ _ _ _ _ _

Step 1: What is your current situation?

Step 2: What are the positives and negative?

Step 3: How does that make you feel?

Step 4: How can the situation be improved?

Date: _ _ _ _ _ _ _ _ _ _ _

Step 1: What is your current situation?

Step 2: What are the positives and negative?

Step 3: How does that make you feel?

Step 4: How can the situation be improved?

Date:_ _ _ _ _ _ _ _ _ _ _

Step 1: What is your current situation?

Step 2: What are the positives and negative?

Step 3: How does that make you feel?

Step 4: How can the situation be improved?

Date: _ _ _ _ _ _ _ _ _ _ _ _

Step 1: What is your current situation?

Step 2: What are the positives and negative?

Step 3: How does that make you feel?

Step 4: How can the situation be improved?

Date: _ _ _ _ _ _ _ _ _ _ _

Step 1: What is your current situation?

Step 2: What are the positives and negative?

Step 3: How does that make you feel?

Step 4: How can the situation be improved?

Date: _ _ _ _ _ _ _ _ _ _

Step 1: What is your current situation?

Step 2: What are the positives and negative?

Step 3: How does that make you feel?

Step 4: How can the situation be improved?

Date: _ _ _ _ _ _ _ _ _ _ _ _

Step 1: What is your current situation?

Step 2: What are the positives and negative?

Step 3: How does that make you feel?

Step 4: How can the situation be improved?

Date: _ _ _ _ _ _ _ _ _ _ _ _ _

Step 1: What is your current situation?

Step 2: What are the positives and negative?

Step 3: How does that make you feel?

Step 4: How can the situation be improved?

Date:_ _ _ _ _ _ _ _ _ _ _ _

Step 1: What is your current situation?

Step 2: What are the positives and negative?

Step 3: How does that make you feel?

Step 4: How can the situation be improved?

Date: _ _ _ _ _ _ _ _ _ _ _

Step 1: What is your current situation?

Step 2: What are the positives and negative?

Step 3: How does that make you feel?

Step 4: How can the situation be improved?

Date: _ _ _ _ _ _ _ _ _ _ _

Step 1: What is your current situation?

Step 2: What are the positives and negative?

Step 3: How does that make you feel?

Step 4: How can the situation be improved?

Date: _ _ _ _ _ _ _ _ _ _ _

Step 1: What is your current situation?

Step 2: What are the positives and negative?

Step 3: How does that make you feel?

Step 4: How can the situation be improved?

Date:_ _ _ _ _ _ _ _ _ _ _

Step 1: What is your current situation?

Step 2: What are the positives and negative?

Step 3: How does that make you feel?

Step 4: How can the situation be improved?

Date:_ _ _ _ _ _ _ _ _ _ _

Step 1: What is your current situation?

Step 2: What are the positives and negative?

Step 3: How does that make you feel?

Step 4: How can the situation be improved?

Date:_ _ _ _ _ _ _ _ _ _ _

Step 1: What is your current situation?

Step 2: What are the positives and negative?

Step 3: How does that make you feel?

Step 4: How can the situation be improved?

Step 1: What is your current situation?

Step 2: What are the positives and negative?

Step 3: How does that make you feel?

Step 4: How can the situation be improved?

Step 1: What is your current situation?

Step 2: What are the positives and negative?

Step 3: How does that make you feel?

Step 4: How can the situation be improved?

Date:_ _ _ _ _ _ _ _ _ _ _

Step 1: What is your current situation?

Step 2: What are the positives and negative?

Step 3: How does that make you feel?

Step 4: How can the situation be improved?

Date:_ _ _ _ _ _ _ _ _ _ _

Step 1: What is your current situation?

Step 2: What are the positives and negative?

Step 3: How does that make you feel?

Step 4: How can the situation be improved?

Date: _ _ _ _ _ _ _ _ _ _ _

Step 1: What is your current situation?

Step 2: What are the positives and negative?

Step 3: How does that make you feel?

Step 4: How can the situation be improved?

Date: _ _ _ _ _ _ _ _ _ _ _ _

Step 1: What is your current situation?

Step 2: What are the positives and negative?

Step 3: How does that make you feel?

Step 4: How can the situation be improved?

Step 1: What is your current situation?

Step 2: What are the positives and negative?

Step 3: How does that make you feel?

Step 4: How can the situation be improved?

Date:_ _ _ _ _ _ _ _ _ _ _

Step 1: What is your current situation?

Step 2: What are the positives and negative?

Step 3: How does that make you feel?

Step 4: How can the situation be improved?

Date: _ _ _ _ _ _ _ _ _ _ _ _

Step 1: What is your current situation?

Step 2: What are the positives and negative?

Step 3: How does that make you feel?

Step 4: How can the situation be improved?

Date: _ _ _ _ _ _ _ _ _ _ _

Step 1: What is your current situation?

Step 2: What are the positives and negative?

Step 3: How does that make you feel?

Step 4: How can the situation be improved?

Step 1: What is your current situation?

Step 2: What are the positives and negative?

Step 3: How does that make you feel?

Step 4: How can the situation be improved?

Date:_ _ _ _ _ _ _ _ _ _

Step 1: What is your current situation?

Step 2: What are the positives and negative?

Step 3: How does that make you feel?

Step 4: How can the situation be improved?

Date:_ _ _ _ _ _ _ _ _ _ _

Step 1: What is your current situation?

Step 2: What are the positives and negative?

Step 3: How does that make you feel?

Step 4: How can the situation be improved?

Date:_ _ _ _ _ _ _ _ _ _ _

Step 1: What is your current situation?

Step 2: What are the positives and negative?

Step 3: How does that make you feel?

Step 4: How can the situation be improved?

Date: _ _ _ _ _ _ _ _ _ _ _

Step 1: What is your current situation?

Step 2: What are the positives and negative?

Step 3: How does that make you feel?

Step 4: How can the situation be improved?

Step 1: What is your current situation?

Step 2: What are the positives and negative?

Step 3: How does that make you feel?

Step 4: How can the situation be improved?

Date:_ _ _ _ _ _ _ _ _ _ _

Step 1: What is your current situation?

Step 2: What are the positives and negative?

Step 3: How does that make you feel?

Step 4: How can the situation be improved?

Step 1: What is your current situation?

Step 2: What are the positives and negative?

Step 3: How does that make you feel?

Step 4: How can the situation be improved?

Date: _ _ _ _ _ _ _ _ _ _ _

Step 1: What is your current situation?

Step 2: What are the positives and negative?

Step 3: How does that make you feel?

Step 4: How can the situation be improved?

Date:_ _ _ _ _ _ _ _ _ _ _

Step 1: What is your current situation?

Step 2: What are the positives and negative?

Step 3: How does that make you feel?

Step 4: How can the situation be improved?

Date: _ _ _ _ _ _ _ _ _ _ _ _

Step 1: What is your current situation?

Step 2: What are the positives and negative?

Step 3: How does that make you feel?

Step 4: How can the situation be improved?

Date: _ _ _ _ _ _ _ _ _ _ _

Step 1: What is your current situation?

Step 2: What are the positives and negative?

Step 3: How does that make you feel?

Step 4: How can the situation be improved?

Date: _ _ _ _ _ _ _ _ _ _ _

Step 1: What is your current situation?

Step 2: What are the positives and negative?

Step 3: How does that make you feel?

Step 4: How can the situation be improved?

Date:_ _ _ _ _ _ _ _ _ _ _

Step 1: What is your current situation?

Step 2: What are the positives and negative?

Step 3: How does that make you feel?

Step 4: How can the situation be improved?

Date:_ _ _ _ _ _ _ _ _ _ _

Step 1: What is your current situation?

Step 2: What are the positives and negative?

Step 3: How does that make you feel?

Step 4: How can the situation be improved?

Date:_ _ _ _ _ _ _ _ _ _ _

Step 1: What is your current situation?

Step 2: What are the positives and negative?

Step 3: How does that make you feel?

Step 4: How can the situation be improved?

Date:_ _ _ _ _ _ _ _ _ _ _

Step 1: What is your current situation?

Step 2: What are the positives and negative?

Step 3: How does that make you feel?

Step 4: How can the situation be improved?

Date:_ _ _ _ _ _ _ _ _ _ _

Step 1: What is your current situation?

Step 2: What are the positives and negative?

Step 3: How does that make you feel?

Step 4: How can the situation be improved?

Step 1: What is your current situation?

Step 2: What are the positives and negative?

Step 3: How does that make you feel?

Step 4: How can the situation be improved?

Date:_ _ _ _ _ _ _ _ _ _ _

Step 1: What is your current situation?

Step 2: What are the positives and negative?

Step 3: How does that make you feel?

Step 4: How can the situation be improved?

Date:_ _ _ _ _ _ _ _ _ _ _

Step 1: What is your current situation?

Step 2: What are the positives and negative?

Step 3: How does that make you feel?

Step 4: How can the situation be improved?

Date:_ _ _ _ _ _ _ _ _ _

Step 1: What is your current situation?

Step 2: What are the positives and negative?

Step 3: How does that make you feel?

Step 4: How can the situation be improved?

Step 1: What is your current situation?

Step 2: What are the positives and negative?

Step 3: How does that make you feel?

Step 4: How can the situation be improved?

Date: _ _ _ _ _ _ _ _ _ _ _ _

Step 1: What is your current situation?

Step 2: What are the positives and negative?

Step 3: How does that make you feel?

Step 4: How can the situation be improved?

Date:_ _ _ _ _ _ _ _ _ _ _

Step 1: What is your current situation?

Step 2: What are the positives and negative?

Step 3: How does that make you feel?

Step 4: How can the situation be improved?

Step 1: What is your current situation?

Step 2: What are the positives and negative?

Step 3: How does that make you feel?

Step 4: How can the situation be improved?

Date:_ _ _ _ _ _ _ _ _ _ _ _

Step 1: What is your current situation?

Step 2: What are the positives and negative?

Step 3: How does that make you feel?

Step 4: How can the situation be improved?

Date:_ _ _ _ _ _ _ _ _ _ _

Step 1: What is your current situation?

Step 2: What are the positives and negative?

Step 3: How does that make you feel?

Step 4: How can the situation be improved?

Date: _ _ _ _ _ _ _ _ _ _ _ _

Step 1: What is your current situation?

Step 2: What are the positives and negative?

Step 3: How does that make you feel?

Step 4: How can the situation be improved?

Date: _ _ _ _ _ _ _ _ _ _ _

Step 1: What is your current situation?

Step 2: What are the positives and negative?

Step 3: How does that make you feel?

Step 4: How can the situation be improved?

Date: _ _ _ _ _ _ _ _ _ _ _ _

Step 1: What is your current situation?

Step 2: What are the positives and negative?

Step 3: How does that make you feel?

Step 4: How can the situation be improved?

Date:_ _ _ _ _ _ _ _ _ _ _

Step 1: What is your current situation?

Step 2: What are the positives and negative?

Step 3: How does that make you feel?

Step 4: How can the situation be improved?

Date:_ _ _ _ _ _ _ _ _ _ _

Step 1: What is your current situation?

Step 2: What are the positives and negative?

Step 3: How does that make you feel?

Step 4: How can the situation be improved?

Step 1: What is your current situation?

Step 2: What are the positives and negative?

Step 3: How does that make you feel?

Step 4: How can the situation be improved?

Date:_ _ _ _ _ _ _ _ _ _

Step 1: What is your current situation?

Step 2: What are the positives and negative?

Step 3: How does that make you feel?

Step 4: How can the situation be improved?

Date:_ _ _ _ _ _ _ _ _ _ _

Step 1: What is your current situation?

Step 2: What are the positives and negative?

Step 3: How does that make you feel?

Step 4: How can the situation be improved?

Date: _ _ _ _ _ _ _ _ _ _ _ _

Step 1: What is your current situation?

Step 2: What are the positives and negative?

Step 3: How does that make you feel?

Step 4: How can the situation be improved?

Date: _ _ _ _ _ _ _ _ _ _ _

Step 1: What is your current situation?

Step 2: What are the positives and negative?

Step 3: How does that make you feel?

Step 4: How can the situation be improved?

Step 1: What is your current situation?

Step 2: What are the positives and negative?

Step 3: How does that make you feel?

Step 4: How can the situation be improved?

Date:_ _ _ _ _ _ _ _ _ _ _

Step 1: What is your current situation?

Step 2: What are the positives and negative?

Step 3: How does that make you feel?

Step 4: How can the situation be improved?

Date: _ _ _ _ _ _ _ _ _ _ _

Step 1: What is your current situation?

Step 2: What are the positives and negative?

Step 3: How does that make you feel?

Step 4: How can the situation be improved?

Date: _ _ _ _ _ _ _ _ _ _ _

Step 1: What is your current situation?

Step 2: What are the positives and negative?

Step 3: How does that make you feel?

Step 4: How can the situation be improved?

Step 1: What is your current situation?

Step 2: What are the positives and negative?

Step 3: How does that make you feel?

Step 4: How can the situation be improved?

Date: _ _ _ _ _ _ _ _ _ _ _

Step 1: What is your current situation?

Step 2: What are the positives and negative?

Step 3: How does that make you feel?

Step 4: How can the situation be improved?

Date: _ _ _ _ _ _ _ _ _ _ _

Step 1: What is your current situation?

Step 2: What are the positives and negative?

Step 3: How does that make you feel?

Step 4: How can the situation be improved?

Step 1: What is your current situation?

Step 2: What are the positives and negative?

Step 3: How does that make you feel?

Step 4: How can the situation be improved?

Date:_ _ _ _ _ _ _ _ _ _ _

Step 1: What is your current situation?

Step 2: What are the positives and negative?

Step 3: How does that make you feel?

Step 4: How can the situation be improved?

Date: _ _ _ _ _ _ _ _ _ _ _ _

Step 1: What is your current situation?

Step 2: What are the positives and negative?

Step 3: How does that make you feel?

Step 4: How can the situation be improved?

Step 1: What is your current situation?

Step 2: What are the positives and negative?

Step 3: How does that make you feel?

Step 4: How can the situation be improved?

Step 1: What is your current situation?

Step 2: What are the positives and negative?

Step 3: How does that make you feel?

Step 4: How can the situation be improved?

Date: _ _ _ _ _ _ _ _ _ _ _ _

Step 1: What is your current situation?

Step 2: What are the positives and negative?

Step 3: How does that make you feel?

Step 4: How can the situation be improved?

Date:_ _ _ _ _ _ _ _ _ _ _ _

Step 1: What is your current situation?

Step 2: What are the positives and negative?

Step 3: How does that make you feel?

Step 4: How can the situation be improved?

Date: _ _ _ _ _ _ _ _ _ _ _

Step 1: What is your current situation?

Step 2: What are the positives and negative?

Step 3: How does that make you feel?

Step 4: How can the situation be improved?

Date:_ _ _ _ _ _ _ _ _ _ _ _

Step 1: What is your current situation?

Step 2: What are the positives and negative?

Step 3: How does that make you feel?

Step 4: How can the situation be improved?

Made in the USA
Las Vegas, NV
27 April 2024